Hapkido:
The Integrated Fighting Art

By Robert K. Spear

UP

DISCLAIMER. Although both Unique Publications and the author(s) of this martial arts book have taken great care to ensure the authenticity of the information and techniques contained herein, we are not responsible, in whole or in part, for any injury which may occur to the reader or readers by reading and/or following the instructions in this publication. We also do not guarantee that the techniques and illustrations described in this book will be safe and effective in a self-defense or training situation. It is understood that there exists a potential for injury when using or demonstrating the techniques herein described. It is essential that before following any of the activities, physical or otherwise, herein described, the reader or readers first should consult his or her physician for advice on whether practicing or using the techniques described in this publication could cause injury, physical or otherwise. Since the physical activities described herein could be too sophisticated in nature for the reader or readers, it is essential a physician be consulted. Also, federal, state or local laws may prohibit the use or possession of weapons described herein. A thorough examination must be made of the federal, state and local laws before the reader or readers attempts to use these weapons in a self-defense situation or otherwise. Neither Unique Publications nor the author(s) of this martial arts book guarantees the legality or the appropriateness of the techniques or weapons herein contained.

ISBN: 0-86568-079-5
Library of Congress Catalog No: 86-50439

Copyright ©1988 by Unique Publications, Inc.
All rights reserved.
Printed in the United States of America.

Designer: Danilo J. Silverio
Editor: John Steven Soet

 **UNIQUE PUBLICATIONS**

4201 Vanowen Place
Burbank, CA 91505

Contents

Part Five: Upper Belt Level Familiarization

Acknowledgements

I would like to express my appreciation to my teacher, Song Ho Jin, Master Ji Han Jae (past president of the Korea Hapkido Association), and to the numerous Korean instructors who so patiently recounted hapkido's history and theories. Thanks also go to the following hapkidoists for their dedicated assistance in the production of this book: to Nelson Ennis and Don Alla-baugh, for serving as demonstrators; and to Bruce Myashiba and Tom Booth, for taking the many photographs necessary for bringing the subject to visual life. Thanks to Professor Don Burns, Indiana University Martial Art Coordinator and President of the United States Hapkido Federation, as well as to Professor Ray Wood, martial art coordinator for the U.S. Military Academy, West Point, for their support and assistance on past hapkido projects. Thanks especially to Bea Wong of Unique Publications for understanding the vision and allowing it to happen.

From left to right: The author's teacher, sixth degree black belt Song Ho Jin; ninth degree Master Ji Han Jae; and the author. The Korea Hapkido Association's main gym is in the background.

Introduction

When I began studying hapkido back in 1973, there were no usable hapkido texts written in English that would serve as a step-by-step guide for advancement. American martial artists are interested in the "why's" as well as the "how to's" of techniques and this knowledge was available only as an oral history. Most of the hundreds of hapkido techniques had no names and were learned by rote memorization of the movements. Theory was generally not taught well because of language/cultural barriers between the Koreans and the Americans. It was then that I vowed to someday write a definitive manual on the art.

Hapkido is a dynamic art, tailored to one's body type, capabilities, and combat situations. It is difficult for one instructor to teach all aspects of the art equally well. For instance, while in Korea I observed that power techniques were best taught by the bigger instructors. Finesse techniques were best taught by the smaller instructors. Because of this, my teacher, Korean Marine Major Song Ho Jin, unselfishly brought in guest instructors of different body types to round out his own approach and our exposure to the many complex aspects of the art. This was unheard of in those days due to the typical inter-instructor rivalry so prevalent among the Orientals. The techniques in this book reflect his universal approach to teaching.

This book outlines examples of the essential techniques for advancement in hapkido as taught by Major Song and required by the Korea Hapkido Association in Seoul, Korea. This was the largest and the only association sanctioned by the Korean Ministry of Education; however, it was one of three different splinter associations. If the order in which the techniques contained within are different from how other hapkidoists learned them, it is probably due to the diversity in organizations. Be not dismayed, however. I have had an opportunity to share knowledge with quite a few hapkidoists since the early 1970s, and have noted that the techniques within were broader in scope than those experienced by Americans who studied elsewhere. Since there are still several hapkido organizations, I have not tried to make it organization specific. The techniques can be easily rearranged to accommodate different belt systems and advancement needs. It should also be noted that as an instructor I find myself further rearranging the order because of different students' needs. The important aspect of this book is that it is just a beginning. There are many variations of these techniques based upon the many different ways their execution can be adjusted. For instance, a certain wrist lock may normally be executed with a spin to the side; however, the situational circumstances may require a step forward or a step backward instead. The many possible adjustments to techniques gives rise to hapkidoists' claims that the art has several thousand techniques. In any case, hapkido *is* a complex art and requires the aid of a qualified instructor.

PART I

Introduction to Hapkido

CHAPTER ONE

The History of Hapkido

A detailed record of hapkido's development through the years is, unfortunately, unchronicled due to a shroud of secrecy placed on it in order for Korean martial arts to survive years of foreign army occupation. Even today, hapkido is just coming into its own in the Republic of Korea. It was only after WWII that its instruction became available to the man on the street. Until that time, only selected Buddhist monks, and before this century, members of nobility were allowed to learn its deadly techniques.

Its earliest developments date back 1300 years to 7th century A.D. during the Silla Dynasty. It was during this period that a group was formed by the ruler Chin Hung. This organization was known as the *Hwa-Rang-Do*, literally translated as "The Way of the Flower Youth." This movement closely paralleled European knighthood in its structure and philosophies. It was composed of young sons of noble families who dedicated their allegiance to the ruling system. They were protectors of the downtrodden and advocates of the martial and intellectual arts. The fighting techniques they developed, although unnamed, were the first evidenced organized martial art study in Korea. Various forms of this fighting system are still found on stone walls and tombs dating back to the Silla Dynasty.

As a class, the Hwa-Rang-Do eventually dissipated into a token set of dandies. The study of fighting techniques slowly disappeared from mainstream noble society but was kept alive, to some extent, in isolated monasteries. It was during this period that there were exchanges of ideas between Korean Buddhist monks and their Chinese counterparts. The Chinese influence is evident in hapkido's circular blocks, its low and spinning kicks, and its heavy emphasis on the mental aspects of concentration and control. During this period, the evolving fighting art gained the name *tae kyun*.

When the Japanese invaded Korea in 1910, they outlawed all Korean martial arts. They did allow the study of Japanese judo and kendo. Tae kyun could only be studied in secret in remote mountain monasteries.

It was shortly after the Japanese occupation's beginning that Choi Yong Suhl (Korean names are formed with the family name first, i.e., Smith John Lee), the originator of modern hapkido, emigrated to Japan. Having already mastered tae kyun in his youth, Master Choi studied a Japanese system called daito ryu or dai ju-jutsu. This system of ju-jutsu is said to be the forerunner of judo and aikido. Master Choi returned to Korea after the end of WWII in 1945, and founded the first hapkido school in Taegu, Korea. Hapkido was an amalgamation of the Chinese-influenced tae kyun and Japanese ju-jutsu. This made it one of the first truly integrated arts that recognized the effectiveness of combining the best aspects of both the "hard" and "soft" styles into very powerful combinations of techniques and theories.

Master Choi acquired some devoted disciples and spent a long time polishing his system into a highly effective means of self-defense specifically designed for the street or battlefield. His training was challenging. Several of his old students relate stories of how they had to dig a large hole in the ground. Periodically they would stop their digging to jump out of the hole without using their hands. When they had dug is as deep as they were able to jump out, they would commence filling it back up and continue jumping out and back until the hole was completely filled up again.

Eventually Master Choi and his top student, Ji Han Jae, brought hapkido to Seoul to teach it to the public for the first time (over 75 percent of the Republic of Korea's population lives in Seoul, making it the logical choice for expansion efforts). Master Choi eventually retired back to Taegu and died in 1987. During Choi's retirement, his life's work was carried on by ninth degree master Ji Han Jae in Seoul as president of the Korea Hapkido Association. At least two other hapkido organizations were started up, one in Seoul and one in Taegu, by other Choi disciples; however, Ji's is the only one that thrived. He became politically well-connected working at the Korean presidential quarters, the Blue House, as the chief martial arts trainer for President Park Chung Hee's 300 Secret Service bodyguards. When not otherwise occupied at the Blue House, Ji supervised the day-to-day operations of the Korea Hapkido Association's main gym in the Seodaemun section of Seoul. After the death of President Park, Ji emigrated to the United States and established a hapkido school in the San Francisco area.

The Philosophy and Application of Hapkido

The Korean term "hapkido" is a combination of three words: "hap," meaning harmony or coordination; "ki," meaning power or more literally, cosmic force; and "do," meaning the way or the art of. In short, hapkido means the art of power coordination.

This coordination of power is manifested in two ways: first and most important is the harmony between the mind and the body. To be able to function most effectively in a combat situation, one must have total control of both mind and body. You should use the physical body as an extension of your mental directives. The second concept of harmony deals with the coordination of an attack or defense. Both concepts are essential to good self-defense. A person might know how to save himself from a knife attack, but if he allows too much fear affect his physical movements in such a way that he becomes clumsy, hurried, or even worse, frozen, then all his knowledge is in vain. Likewise a person may be totally calm, in full control of his emotions and body; however, if he does not know how to use his opponent's movements and force, he will be at a disadvantage.

The Koreans describe this harmony or coordination of power on a deeper, more philosophical level. Being greatly influenced by both Buddhism and Taoism, they feel that hapkido is a way of becoming one with nature. This is a concept central to both of these Chinese influences.

Although hapkido is primarily defensive in nature, it can be very offensive when the need arises. Many of its techniques are based upon an opponent's attack. Once the attack has been nullified (or even simultaneously to the attack), a devastating counterattack is launched. Some people try to compare hapkido directly to Japanese aikido, which uses similar joint bending techniques and throws. One reason for this comparison is that the Japanese *kanji* figures for aikido and the Korean figures for hapkido are exactly alike and translate into the same English words: the art of power coordination/harmony. In actuality, hapkido continues to a point beyond that reached by aikido in its philosophy of self-defense. According to Yoshitsu Yamada in his book *Complete Aikido*, an aikidoist will apply defensive techniques only, nullifying attack after attack until the aggressor becomes thoroughly confused and frustrated and gives up. Hapkido not only meets the attack, but turns it back against the opponent and follows through with offensive methods which may control his violence or may render him incapable of living, much less being capable of any further antagonistic actions.

The element of self-control is very important in situations requiring self-defense. For example, one would react differently to a drunken friend at a party than he would to a mugger on a dark street. In the first instance, he may want to constrain his friend so that no one is harmed. In the second, he may be fighting for his life and, therefore, he might find it necessary to kill or be killed. Hapkido teaches techniques of many different levels of harshness. It also teaches when to use them.

Hapkido's basic techniques consist of kicking, striking, joint-breaking throws and locks, both soft and hard blocks, nerve and muscle pressure attacks, and self-defense skills with common weapons such as the walking cane and the 12″ billy club.

The most important element in hapkido and one of the most difficult to develop is the power of the mind. The basis for mental power is **ki**. Ki is an Oriental concept of the power in nature all around us. It is said that all living things possess ki in varying intensities. Perhaps one could say that plants express ki when they give off measurable reactions to human emotions directed toward them in scientific tests.

Martial artists say that one can tap into this essence of force around us and use it as one's own. They cite examples of hysterical strength and similar superhuman feats of speed and power as proof.

Whether the body performs feats far beyond its normal capabilities for short periods of time because of help from an external natural force or because governor-like mental blocks have been temporarily stripped away is not as important as the fact that the human body is capable of superhuman feats. This ability can be consciously developed. The ideal to strive for is the ability to understand the power of ki, to learn how to draw upon it, and to use it at will. Three hapkido concepts may be used as tools for positive ki control:

1. *Mind-Like-Water* is a vital concept to many martial arts. The most effective mind, especially in a combat situation, is one that is totally free of emotion, free to center its attention on the task at hand. Ideally, one's mind should be like a pool of water that is placid, undisturbed, at rest. Allow one violent, uncontrolled emotion to enter the mind and it's as if a rock had been dropped into the quiet pool. The whole surface becomes disturbed and concentration will be lost as a result. Without total concentration, ki cannot be coordinated or focused. When one loses concentration, he also loses his initiative. If one's life and well-being are endangered, he must not allow anger or fear to disturb his concentration. People who have learned to do this become fighting machines, feeling no fear or pain until the combat has finished. They are capable of hearing and seeing more, moving faster and more powerfully, and sense reality as a slow motion film.

2. Only if you develop a mind-like-water can you develop the second ability called the *mind-like-moon* (aikidoists call it "soft eyes.") This concept emphasizes total awareness in all directions. The moon bathes the landscape with a serene, all-knowing light. Ki extends our awareness in all directions if we but learn to recognize its signals. Another exercise we do in our class is a ki sensing exercise with our eyes closed. The students are taught to feel an aura around them that some describe as a feeling of static electricity. When a person or object gets too close to that aura, a disturbance is felt. Naturally, a high degree of concentration is required to learn this, plus the guidance of an experienced instructor who not only knows how to do this but also knows how to guide students into realizing the capability lies within them. With the mind-like-moon, one may have a better opportunity to sense danger, threats, and openings in combat.

3. Distinctly characteristic of both hapkido and aikido, is the concept of the *live-hand*. Open one hand as wide as possible. Notice how hard the wrist and forearm become. Hapkidoists believe that this wide-open hand gathers ki in from the air, which in turn flows through the arm and chest down into the *tanjon* (*tan tien* in Chinese). This is an area approximately three inches

in diameter centered just below the navel. The tanjon is the spiritual center of power in the body for the Koreans. They believe that since this is where all the nourishment and power enters an unborn baby's body, the same should hold true for an adult. Spiritual aspects aside, the tanjon area is the power center in a physical sense as well. One's center of gravity lies in this region and it is also the point where the major muscle groups of the body directly or indirectly interconnect. Tapping into ki with the live-hand and pouring it into the tanjon will ensure this power will be used throughout the body in a coordinated manner.

Prove to yourself the surprising strength of the live-hand. Hold an arm straight out in front, making a fist with the thumb area on the top and the little finger on the bottom. Ask a friend to pull down on your upper arm with one hand and to push up on your fist with the other, trying to bend your arm while you resist and try to keep it straight. Unless unusually strong, most people find their arm being bent. Now repeat the experiment except, instead of using a fist, this time open out your hand completely and imagine ki flowing through it. You will find that as long as you concentrate on the ki flow, your arm cannot be bent.

Principles of Motion

The techniques of hapkido are based on two dynamic theories:

1. Theory of spinning (turning or redirection of force).

2. Theory of joining and one step (using your opponent's force in conjunction with your own).

The theory of spinning implies circular movement and it is in this sense that hapkido is a "soft" art. Rather than meet a blow head-on, hapkido teaches that the blow should be redirected in a direction less harmful to the defender. This is done by changing a straight-line blow into a more rounded or circular movement around or past the intended target. The theory of spinning is also applied for throws and for those hapkido kicks and strikes which are based upon centrifugal force.

The theory of joining and one step is concerned with taking advantage of an opponent's force and adding one's own force to the counter to the opponent's detriment. For instance, an attacker throws a right cross at your face. Quickly stepping to your left (or his right), push his right elbow slightly toward the center (theory of spinning) causing him to miss his target (your face). In the meantime, he will continue to move forward under the impetus of his attack. If you should follow through after your first defensive movement (one step) and counterattack with a blow to his face while he is still moving forward, you will *join* his force and your own together and the sum total of the two forces will culminate at the point in time when your hand meets his unguarded face. Later on, we will see how this concept is applied in numerous hapkido counterattacks.

Water Theory

Hapkido fighting strategy, as developed by Master Ji Han Jae, is known was water theory. It consists of three aspects. The first is based upon the concept that water exerts pressure on everything in contact with it. A hapkidoist learns how to exert constant pressure upon his opponent by using combinations of speed, movement, and distancing. For this reason, hapkido is excellent for in-fighting. When opposing an opponent, you can move inside an attack, thereby creating pressure on him. By increasing the fight tempo at that instant, you can quickly capitalize on his temporary vulnerability, manipulating his countering movements with your own attack. The hapkidoist applies constant pressure on his opponent. He always strives to anticipate his opponent's attack options and then limits them by movement. The opponent is controlled and manipulated as the hapkidoist changes his position, fighting distance, and fight tempo.

The second aspect of water theory is that water always has some influence on anything it contacts. It either makes things wet or wears them away. If a person wants to swim (fight), he has to get wet (accept the consequences). The hapkidoist learns to make an assailant's attack so costly that he will think twice before trying it again. We normally think defensively in the martial arts, i.e., neutralize the attack then counterattack. Hapkido, on the other hand, also attempts to create pain or injuries while blocking so that the attack is neutralized and countered simultaneously. The primary method by which this is done is by blocking against painful pressure points. By blocking against a pressure point on an attacking limb, you can disrupt the attack, create an opening, and/or render the limb useless. These points are described later on in this chapter.

The third aspect of water theory is related to water's weight and momentum. If a submarine springs a small leak, the pressure of the surrounding water will force the water into the small hole so hard that the hole will become larger and larger. In the same manner, the hapkidoist looks for an opening, attacks it, and follows through with stronger and more effective techniques. It is like a chess game where one thinks several moves ahead. Each technique creates other openings which, in turn, invite further techniques. From this aspect comes the idea of combat flow.

The constant emphasis on sensing and taking advantage of combat flow requires a different training approach from traditional martial arts' rote memorization of forms. *Kata, hyung*, and other forms do not take into consideration that attacks and counterattacks vary in their angles, timing, and intensity. A rising block, for example, may not always be effective against an overhead strike. If the strike is too strong, you may have to change from a rising block to a deflection block to the side in mid-technique. There is no way that forms can teach this adjustment to the combat flow. A methodology that does work is A) teaching numerous technique options, B) talking through fight scenario sequences in slow motion, C) having two students each talk through their attacks and counterattacks in slow motion until they are able to maintain a steady flow of techniques without hesitation, and D) gradually pick up the speed until all the techniques are going at full speed and yet are under control to prevent injuries.

A knowledge of the human body's strengths, weaknesses, and capabilities is essential to hapkido. A firm foundation in knowledge of vulnerable targets is needed in order that the defendent may bring his attacker under control in the most expedient manner. A vital spot is any part or point on the body vulnerable to attack. Figures 2-1 and 2-2 depict 54 basic vital points studied by hapkidoists.

1. the temples
2. the eyes
3. the ear holes
4. above the bridge of the nose
5. cheek bones
6. tip of the nose
7. nerve point between the nose and lips
8. nerve points under ear lobes
9. chin
10. carotid arteries
11. larynx
12. subclavian nerves between collar bone and neck
13. collar bones
14. esophagus
15. sternum
16. heart
17. solar plexus
18. ribs
19. short ribs
20. tanjon
21. groin
22. genitalia
23. nerve point between bicep and tricep
23-A. arm pit
24. top of the forearm muscle
25. nerve point inside elbow
26. nerve point on top of wrist
27. tendon point on top of two tendons in inner wrist
28. nerve point between thumb and first finger
29. tendons on backs of hands
30. nerve point between middle and ring finger knuckles

31. inner thighs
32. tendon connection points above
    and below knees
33. knee cap
34. side of knee joint
35. shin bone
36. front of ankle
37. outside of ankle
38. inner ankle
39. top of feet
40. base of skull-neck junction
41. back and sides of neck

42. underneath the shoulder blades
43. upper spine
44. ribs
45. kidneys
46. mid spine
47. lower spine
48. coccyx (tail bone)
49. behind and above the point of the elbow
50. hamstring muscles
51. behind the knees
52. calves
53. Achilles tendon

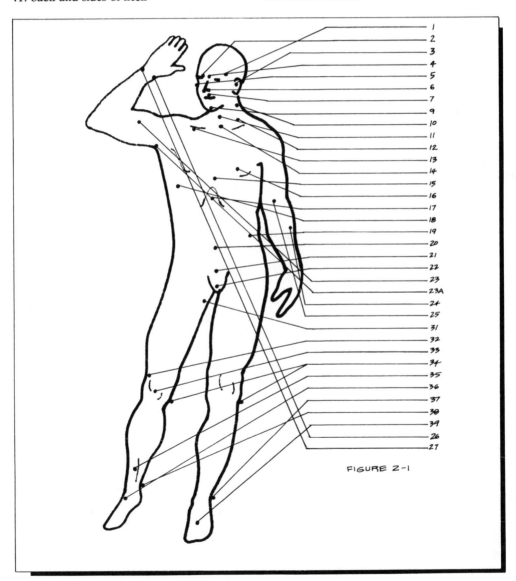

FIGURE 2-1

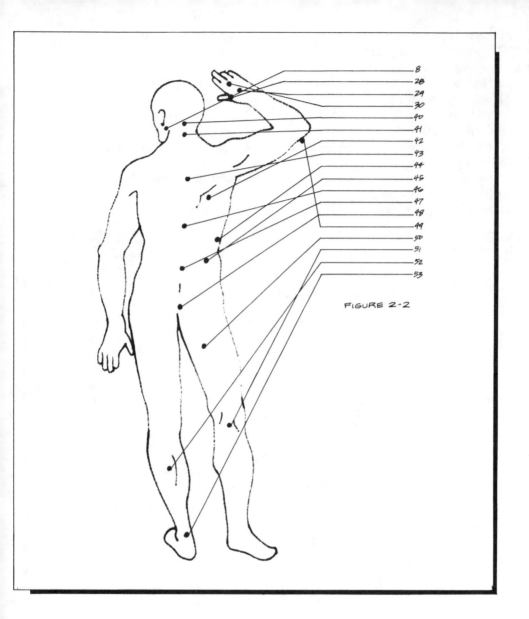

FIGURE 2-2

8
28
29
30
40
41
42
43
44
45
46
47
48
49
50
51
52
53

Training

If you are not currently studying a martial art or participating in any strenuous sport, you should get a good physical examination from a physician before undertaking hapkido. If you're a weekend golfer or bowler and sit at a desk the rest of the week doing no other exercise, it can be decidedly uncomfortable and quite likely dangerous to commence a rigorous training schedule without adequate preparation and a medical examination. A cardinal rule to remember upon venturing into any vigorous sport is "train, don't strain." If you are *really* out of shape, it might be best if you take it easy the first couple of weeks. A capable instructor should minimize the danger of overtraining your body during the early weeks of instruction. It usually takes two to three weeks to build up your body to a point when aches, pains and stiffness are minimal. Remember that you are the best judge of your own endurance and pain levels during the first few weeks. However, you will only get out of hapkido what you put into it. Expect to experience some pain; sometimes it is necessary in order to properly learn certain techniques. The first rule of hapkido is "without pain, there is no gain."

There are a number of general guidelines or axioms to observe when studying hapkido. These guidelines may be augmented by your instructor to allow for local conditions.

Class Rules

1. Learning equals pain. (You have to experience some of the pain of a technique to truly understand its effectiveness.)

2. Strict obedience and attention will be given to the instructor at all times. The instructor's word is law.

3. Proper courtesies must be observed. Salute (bow) to the flag upon entering or leaving the *dojang* (gym), to the instructor at the beginning and end of class and to one another at the beginning and end of a free-sparring session.

4. Absolutely no horseplay or unsupervised free-sparring while in the dojang.

5. Breaches of discipline and concentration should be punished by additional exercises as prescribed by the instructor.

6. If the instructor claps his hands, give him your full attention.

7. Students should begin practice with a clean *tobok* (uniform).

8. Any injury, no matter how minor, should be reported to the instructor immediately.

9. Students will clean the dojang when directed.

10. Students will not sit or lie down unless told to do so by the instructor.

11. Hapkido can be lethal and therefore should not be used on the street except in dire emergencies; it is a last resort when talking or running away have proved impossible.

12. Students will not argue with students of other martial arts (tae kwon do, judo, etc.) as to which one is best. All arts have strong and weak points and should be mutually respected.

13. Students should not be boastful or bullying. They have an obligation to protect other people in danger.

Uniform

Although a uniform is not absolutely essential to the study of hapkido, it is recommended that students procure a heavy tobok or gi, such as is used in judo. This is stronger and will last longer than the lightweight karate outfit. This is especially important because for some hapkido throws, you will grab an opponent's clothing. The lighter weight outfits tend to rip too easily. Toboks can usually be purchased through your instructor, from sporting goods stores, or ordered from advertisements in martial arts magazines.

Schedule

Training schedules will vary because of instructors' availability and students' free time; however, I feel that the optimum benefits come from an alternate-day time table. Rather than working out for an hour every day, it is better to work out for 2-2 ½ hours every other day. This schedule is based on the old weight lifting theory of tearing down the muscles one day and allowing them to rebuild and rest the next day. Practicing every day tends to be boring and leads to a feeling of staleness.

Dojang

Hapkido requires little in the way of equipment or training facilities. The only thing essential to its study is a mat on which to practice break-falls and throws. Some nice-to-have items are:

1. A large wall mirror so students can observe their form or technique.

2. A hand-held kicking target made out of rubber tire sections wrapped with an old inner tube and attached to a wooden handle.

3. A heavy suspended punching/kicking bag.

4. Various knives and clubs made from wood or rubber to use in self-defense practice.

5. Leg and arm weights to increase strength and speed.

6. Various protective padding for use in full-contact free-sparring.

The gym should be large enough to permit freedom of movement. It should also be well-lit and airy to provide a proper atmosphere for practice. During good weather, periodic practices should be held outdoors to lend realism to the training. Students should become familiar with hapkido techniques performed on uneven ground and unsure footing to ensure that these factors will not detract from their performance in a life-or-death situation.

Selecting a Gym

Choosing a gym or training school that best suits you as a student is very important. The instructors should not only know the art, they should be able to impart that knowledge. As is true in other sports, the best players don't always make the best coaches. One should look for an instructor who is dedicated to the art and its principles and who shows a real concern for his students' progress and safety. Instructors have to make a living like anyone else; however, they should not "sell" the belts. Advancement should be earned! In Korea, one usually must be a fourth degree black belt in order to become an instructor. This ensures that the instructor has sufficient experience to teach all aspects of the art. Unfortunately, very few stateside instructors have attained this high a rank, but don't let this discourage you. There are quite a few lower ranked black belts who have adequate experience, the ability to teach, and a dedication to the art, which make them excellent instructors.

Belt System

As in most other martial arts, hapkido uses a system of colored belts to indicate a student's progress. In the Replublic of Korea, belts are ranked as follows:

White: novice

Blue: beginner

Red: intermediate

Black: advanced; first through ninth dan (expert through master)

Depending on the individual instructor, the ranks may be broken down further within the belts.

White Belt Requirement Show up for class.

Blue Belt Requirements

Advancement is based upon performance and achievement tests given by qualified instructors. To be promoted to this rank a student should have mastered basic techniques. Students should have at least three months' experience before they are allowed to free spar.

Red Belt Requirements

A student should be tested on his knowledge of intermediate techniques. He should also prove his ability in free-sparring against his contemporaries and superiors.

First Degree Black Belt Requirements

The student should be familiar with all the basic and intermediate concepts. He should demonstrate this knowledge and free spar against his contemporaries and superiors.

Second Degree Black Belt Requirements

The student must know counters to all the techniques required for first degrees and perform some of the jumping-spinning kicks as well as certain other advanced moves. He should also know the fighting-stick techniques.

Third Degree Black Belt Requirements

The student should be knowledgeable of the umbrella/cane techniques and quarter-staff fighting.

Fourth Degree Black Belt Requirements

The student should be knowledgeable of the bamboo sword, certain self-defense techniques with a handkerchief, and be able to demonstrate an ability to teach.

Fifth Through Ninth Degree Black Belt Requirements

These are honorary degrees, based on time-in-grade, years of study, and teaching experience.

It is important to note that the following chapters only offer examples of the techniques contained in the various ranks. Hapkido is so complex no book could even begin to undertake a detailed analysis of all techniques.

PART II

Basics: Blue Belt

Warm-up Exercises

Before participating in any strenuous sport, you should always warm-up. You must stretch your muscles and tendons gradually to minimize the possibility of strains, sprains, or tears. In the work-out sessions conducted in Korea, hapkidoists use the following sets of exercises for pre-practice warm-ups and general body conditioning.

Tanjon Breathing

One of the most important means of strengthening and relaxing the abdominal muscles is a set of deep-breathing/isometric exercises, which also stretch the inner thighs and increase lung capacity. If done correctly, these exercises will leave you coated with a fine film of perspiration and noticeably looser.

Fig. 5-1

There are four sets of tanjon breathing. First, stand with legs spread wider than shoulder width, knees slightly bent, buttocks positioned above your heels with your hips pushed forward and shoulders back (fig. 5-1). The hands should be wide-spread in the "live-hand" position (fig. 5-2). Take a *deep* breath through the nose and try to push it down into the groin. Of course it won't really go there but trying to push it there will tense the appropriate muscle groups. While holding the breath, lower your body straight down and slowly force the hands out to the front as in (fig. 5-3). When this extension is reached, slowly come back to the starting position, exhaling through the mouth. Repeat immediately without taking shallow breaths between repetitions. Do a total of five repetitions.

Fig. 5-2

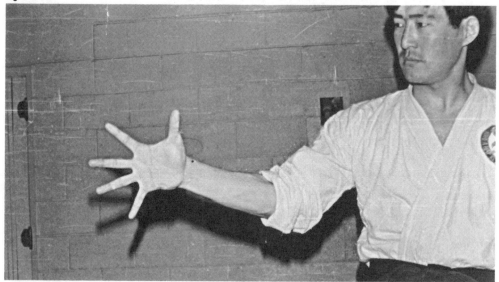

Fig. 5-3

The second set starts the same way except that the arms are held out at the sides (fig. 5-4). Using the same breathing technique, slowly force your hands inward to the center (fig. 5-5) and then return to the beginning. Do five reps.

Fig. 5-4

Fig. 5-5

The third set begins like the first but the hands travel upward (fig. 5-6) to an overhead extension (fig. 5-7). While doing this, pretend that you're pushing the moon up into the sky. Do five reps.

Fig. 5-6

Fig. 5-7

The fourth set, also done five times, starts as in (fig. 5-8) and moves downward to the position shown in (fig. 5-9); think of pushing the moon down. While you hold your breath on all of these, concentrate on pushing your stomach as far out as possible against your belt. Do not try to puff your chest out! Strangely enough, the stomach muscles will become tight and the chest will expand on its own over a period of weeks.

Fig. 5-8

Fig. 5-9

Doing the tanjon breathing exercises helps you to stretch your body and encourages you to use the lower lung lobes which, as any yoga practitioner can tell you, is important for a healthy body. Also important is the added strength the abdomen acquires, which will help protect you from internal injuries caused by kicks or blows to that region. In addition, strengthening the tanjon area will increase the speed and power of both kicks and punches, since this area controls the major body movements and serves as an interconnecting link between the upper and lower body.

Basic
Kicking Techniques

Like all other Korean fighting arts, hapkido places heavy emphasis on kicking techniques. There are some similarities between hapkido kicks and tae kwon do kicks, but there are also many differences. To a certain extent, hapkido bridges the gap between Korean and Japanese arts in that it incorporates throwing and locking techniques with kicks and blows; however, certain aspects of its kicking system are unlike any of those in either country.

Probably the greatest area of dissimilarity is hapkido's "follow-through" kicks, as opposed to "one-point-focus" kicks. Instead of focusing a kick at a certain point just to the rear of a target, hapkido goes one step beyond. It applies its natural and circular movement concepts and extends the focal point to infinity. The essential thought of "thinking through" the target is still present; however, hapkido raises the question of why should one stop at *any* particular point? Since the whole point of thinking through the target is to ensure that the subconscious mind does not slow the blow prior to impact because of anticipation and fear of contact, hapkidoists feel that any stopping point short of a natural limb extension or a completed arc of a circle might unintentionally bring about that very slow-down that we are trying to avoid.

The idea of natural movements and positions cannot be over-stressed. So often beginning students strain to perform certain kicks and are not able to do so. The key remedy is "controlled relaxation." If one relaxes, it becomes much easier to throw the foot in the manner that the mind is telling it to move. Controlled relaxation is essential to the hapkido kick's snap-power. Most practitioners of other martial arts utilize snap-power when they execute a good reverse punch. The fist moves forward, palm facing up, until it is immediately in front of the target, then it suddenly turns over and explodes all of its kinetic energy at once. The same technique can be used for kicking. Many hapkido kicks suddenly pick up speed just before they make contact. This snapping power performs two functions. It greatly increases the force of the kick, and it helps to throw off an opponent's timing for any block attempts. To perform a good, snappy kick one must be limber and concentrate on following through. Can you imagine a golfer or a batter trying to stop his swing at a focal point just past the point of contact (excluding bunting) of their respective targets?

One of the most important muscle groups that gives a kick plenty of snap is the tanjon area or abdominal muscles. This is one of the reasons we seek to strengthen the tanjon by means of the deep breathing exercises. The tanjon is an essential link in the chain of nerve/muscle sequences required for good kicking.

There are two basic classes of kicks in hapkido: elementary, which includes mostly single kicks; and advanced, which include double kicks and jumping kicks. A familiarity with the first class is required for the attainment of blue belt. A partial summary of these kicks follows.

Front Kick:

From the starting position (fig. 6-1) bring the kicking leg's knee up straight until the thigh is parallel to the floor (fig. 6-2). Note how the toes are pointed. Of course kicking barefooted at anything with the toes pointed like that would hurt; however, in most cases on the street, one would be wearing shoes. The pointed toes are essential to step number two as shown in (fig. 6-3). Snap the lower leg out, striking with the toes, and at the same time, thrust your hips forward. This last action adds power and extends the normal range of the kick to an unexpected distance. Return the leg so that it cannot be caught by the opponent. All these actions should be done smoothly. The target is the groin, tanjon, throat, or face.

Fig. 6-1

Fig. 6-2

Fig. 6-3

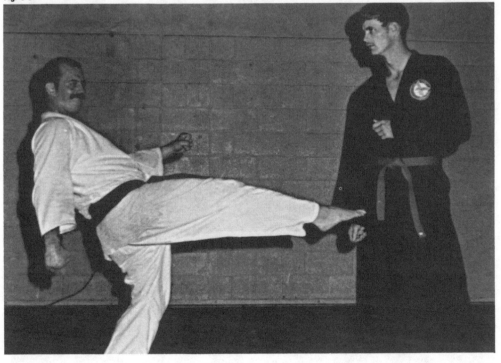

Side Kick (Low Point):

From the starting position, raise your knee across your body and angle the kicking foot's outside edge slightly downward (fig. 6-4). Thrust the foot outward and down to a full leg-extension (fig. 6-5), striking the opponent just above the knee. This will break his knee joint.

Fig. 6-4

Fig. 6-5

Side Kick (Mid Point):

This is a difficult kick and requires much practice. Unlike the low side kick, the knee comes straight up from the starting position (just like a front kick) to the position shown in (fig. 6-6 front view). Keeping the knee to the front, without letting it travel across the body, pivot on the supporting leg. Shoot the leg and hip forward so that the outside edge of the foot, (fig. 6-7 side view) or the heel, strikes the target (fig. 6-8). Aim at the tanjon, short ribs, solar plexus, or kidney areas.

Fig. 6-6

Fig. 6-7

Fig. 6-8

Side Kick (High Point):

As in the previous kick (fig. 6-9), bring the knee straight up, pivot and shoot the leg and hip forward and up high to full extension (fig. 6-10). Return the leg to a cocked position (fig. 6-11). Targets for this kick are the face, head, and throat.

Fig. 6-9

Fig. 6-10

Fig. 6-11

Back Side Kick:

From a comfortable stance raise your leg (fig. 6-12) and thrust backward to a full extension (fig. 6-13). Targets are the groin, body, or face and neck area.

Fig. 6-12

Fig. 6-13

Inside Crescent Kick:

Raise your knee chest-high to the outside (fig. 6-14), then snap the foot straight across in front of your body (fig. 6-15). The target is the head or face or it may be used as a block.

Note that the leg must be relaxed and flexed. *Do not* use the stiff leg taught in other arts since that slows the movement and takes away from the kick's force.

Fig. 6-14　　　　　　　　　　　　　　　　　　**Fig. 6-15**

Outside Crescent Kick

Raise your knee across your body at chest height (fig. 6-16). Unleash the leg back across the body toward the outside, bringing the kicking foot by at face level (fig. 6-17). The weapon, the outside edge of the foot, can practically rip a man's face off. It may also be used as a block against punches or kicks.

Fig. 6-16

Fig. 6-17

Shin Bone Kick

Raise your foot up and back (fig. 6-18) and thrust through to a natural extension at a low point with your foot pointing sideways (fig. 6-19). A strike in the shin by the inside edge of the foot can be excruciating, while a strike to the ankle or just below the front of the knee can break your adversary's leg.

Fig. 6-18

Fig. 6-19

Knife Foot Pivot Kick

Step forward with your left foot at a 90-degree angle to your body (fig. 6-20). Raise the right knee and foot up and to the side (fig. 6-21). Swing the foot through in a natural arc with the outside, or knife, edge of the foot as a weapon (fig. 6-22). Continue the arc until your body is facing one quarter turn to the left of its starting position (fig. 6-23). The cutting edge of the foot is raked across the opponent's knees, thighs, or groin.

Fig. 6-20

Fig. 6-21

Fig. 6-22

Fig. 6-23

Heel-Down Kick

Of hapkido's bag of tricks, this technique is one of the most brutally devastating. It is used as a *coup-de-grace* or a finishing touch. The heel-down kick is used after the opponent has already been disabled to some extent. It is most often used in conjunction with a front kick. For instance, when an adversary is attacked by a front kick to the groin, he will normally bend over clutching his painfully injured privates. At that instance continue the attack with the heel-down kick. Circle his bent body to your inside (fig. 6-24) bringing your foot up as high as possible (fig. 6-25), and drive the heel straight down on his head or spine (fig. 6-26) as fast and as hard as you can. When practicing this kick, raise up on the toes of the supporting leg so that you won't hit the floor with your heel as it swings through to the rear.

Fig. 6-24

Fig. 6-25

Fig. 6-26

Breakfalls

One of the most important skills you will gain from studying hapkido is learning to fall safely. The breakfall system used in hapkido is essentially the same as in judo. Your natural instinct when falling is to try to catch yourself by sticking out a hand. That is probably the worst possible action to take. At the moment of impact all your body weight and inertia are concentrated at the hand and arm doing the catching. This usually will produce a sprained wrist at best and a broken wrist, elbow, or dislocated shoulder at worst.

The best way to break a fall is to distribute the impact force over a wide area simultaneously. Think of a man trying to cross very thin ice. If he walks normally, too much of his body weight will be concentrated in one place and the ice will break. If he lies down on the ice, spreading his weight over a large area, the thin ice may support him.

The same theory holds true for falling: spread the weight over a large area to absorb the force of the fall.

Breakfall No. 1

Sit on the mat with your legs extended straight to the front. Cross your arms upon your chest and place your chin upon your chest (fig. 7-1 & 2). Throw yourself backward, bringing your legs

Fig. 7-1

up and keeping your chin tucked into your chest. This will keep your head from hitting the floor. At the instant before your midback makes contact with the mat, sharply snap your arms outward and downward so that the palms of your hands slap the mat at the same time your back touches the mat (fig. 7-3). It is very important that your arms come out at a 45-degree angle to your body and not straight out. If they come out too wide, it's possible to dislocate the shoulders. This is the proper breakfall for landing flat on your back safely.

Fig. 7-2

Fig. 7-3

Breakfall No. 2

Lie on your right hip with your chin on your chest, right arm on the mat at a 45-degree angle to the body, right leg bent and flat, left hand across the stomach, and left leg bent with knee pointed toward the ceiling (fig. 7-4). This is the correct position for landing safely on one's right side. The position for a left-side landing is shown in (fig. 7-5) as the exact opposite position. To practice this breakfall throw yourself from side to side, slapping the mat with the hand that is out (figs. 7-6 through 7-8).

Fig. 7-4

Fig. 7-5

Fig. 7-6

Fig. 7-7

Fig. 7-8

Breakfall No. 3

To land properly while taking a nosedive is simply a matter of learning to roll with the fall. An easy way to begin learning this technique is to place the right foot forward, raise the right arm, and point the palm of the left hand downward as shown in (fig. 7-9).

Bend forward till the left palm and the back of the right hand touch the mat (fig. 7-10).

Roll straight forward, keeping the head tucked in (fig. 7-11). As you land on your left hip, slap the mat hard with the left hand (fig. 7-12). Notice that you're now in the correct position of a left-side fall. Repeat the process on the other side using the opposite limbs.

Fig. 7-9

Fig. 7-10

Fig. 7-11

Fig. 7-12

Breakfall No. 4

A more advanced form of side-breakfalls starts at a standing position (fig. 7-13). Bring your right foot and hand across your body (fig. 7-14) and fall to the side (fig. 7-15), landing in the right side-fall position while slapping the mat (fig. 7-16). The opposite directions apply for a left side fall.

Fig. 7-13

Fig. 7-14

Fig. 7-15

Fig. 7-16

Practice these falling techniques until they become completely automatic. The instinct to reach out an arm to catch yourself must be totally overcome. Thirty to fifty repetitions of the basic falls per practice session, and the same number of repetitions of the more advanced ones later on, is not unreasonable. The ability to do these breakfalls instinctively could save your life. It will surely help prevent serious injury during hapkido throwing practice and free-sparring sessions.

Basic Strikes

Many parts of the body may be used as weapons for striking an assailant. One of the more natural ones is the fist. Fig. 8-1 shows the correct way to make a fist for maximum damage to an attacker and minimum harm to oneself. The fingers should be curled tightly and the top of the hand should be in a straight line with the wrist and arm. Bending the wrist may result in spraining or breaking it when you deliver a punch. The large knuckles of the first two fingers are the specific points of contact with the target.

Fig. 8-1

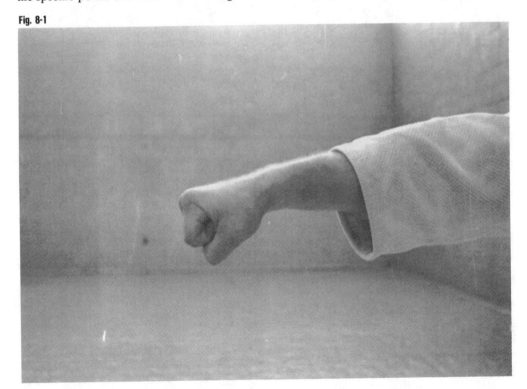

Figures 8-2 through 5 demonstrate the correct way to use the fist in a reverse punch. The fist comes from the side and the other hand starts from in front (fig. 8-2). The fist moves forward while the other hand moves backward (fig. 8-3) creating a spring-like tension across the tanjon, chest, and shoulder muscles. As the fist reaches the two-thirds point of its travel, it starts to turn (fig. 8-4). This turning creates a corkscrew effect which will cause the knuckles to tear and cut the flesh of your opponent. The correct position of the fist at its extension is shown in (fig. 8-5).

Fig. 8-2

Fig. 8-3

Fig. 8-4

Fig. 8-5

Figures 8-6 through 8 show the reverse punch being used at an upward angle.

The hand strikes in this art cover every conceivable method of the human hand striking another surface, and are limited only by the imagination of the practitioner. Some examples of the more popular strikes are the hammer fist (fig. 8-9), the palm heel strike (fig. 8-10), the edge of hand (chop) blow (fig. 8-11) and the forearm smash (fig. 8-12).

Fig. 8-6

Fig. 8-7

Fig. 8-8

Fig. 8-9

Fig. 8-10

Fig. 8-11

Fig. 8-12

Hitting Techniques

There are three major divisions of self-defense techniques required for attaining blue belt. This section addresses the first division, using a hitting technique to escape an assailant who is holding your wrist. The other two divisions also address wristhold escapes. The reason only wrist escapes are taught at the blue belt level is that you can use many of these techniques when being grabbed elsewhere on the body.

Throughout all the sections on self-defense, much stress will be placed on the live-hand principle. It is essential to most of these techniques. For instance, let's say someone comes up and grabs your right wrist with his left hand and starts to hit you in the face with his right fist. If he's strong, you may not be able to pull your hand away even if you pull away against the thumb side of his hand. However, you will be able to escape if you use the live-hand. Tensing the live-hand will harden and expand the wrist, making it easy to pull your hand away. But, why only pull your hand away if you can use it against your opponent? Let's take a look at the first eight blue belt self-defense techniques and see just how an assailant's actions might be used against him.

Escape No. 1

As soon as your wrist is grabbed, tense the live-hand as shown in (fig. 9-1). This will hold true in every wrist escape.

Turn to the left, grabbing the assailant's left wrist (fig. 9-2). Pull his arm high and pull your hand free, maintaining the live-hand (fig. 9-3). Snap your right elbow into his armpit, which is a major nerve center (fig. 9-4). Done hard enough, this blow should numb his entire arm and possibly dislocate his shoulder.

Fig. 9-1

Fig. 9-2

54

Fig. 9-3

Fig. 9-4

55

Retaining his wrist, bring your elbow out of his armpit and place the bottom edge of your forearm against a point just above his left elbow (fig. 9-5), and press smoothly and firmly downward (fig. 9-6). This will result in great pain since the elbow joint will be hyperextended. If you hit, instead of pushing against the elbow joint, it will shatter. This type of injury is excruciatingly painful and should put an attacker out of commission.

Fig. 9-5

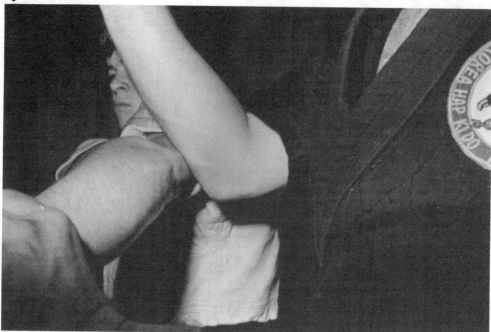

Fig. 9-6

Escape No. 2

This next movement is a little easier than the first but is not as deadly. Simply turn to the right, raising your opponent's left arm and draw your left arm back (fig. 9-7). Without lunging your body, uncross your arms. This action will pull your opponent toward you while your left elbow buries itself in his left armpit (fig. 9-8).

Fig. 9-7

Fig. 9-8

Escape No. 3

Swing your left hand downward and strike the top of your opponent's left wrist, where a major nerve center lies, with a glancing blow from the bony bottom of your left wrist (figs. 9-9 through 11). Immediately reverse your motion and bring a knife-hand into his neck (fig. 9-12) where it joins with the skull. This blow can kill; however, if you lower the striking point one inch it willl only stun him.

Fig. 9-9

Fig. 9-10

Fig. 9-11

Fig. 9-12

59

Joint Lock
Self-Defense Techniques

Although some of these next techniques are somewhat more difficult to perform than those in the previous section, they have the advantage of split-second control and can be modified to fit different situations by inflicting differing degrees of pain. The difference between breaking a joint or simply immobilizing it with pain is determined by the speed and force one puts into these counters. As in the hitting techniques, the locks are very dependent on the proper use of the live-hand.

Joint Lock No. 1

Push the live-hand inward (fig. 10-1) to loosen your opponent's grip. Note the space between the attacker's palm and the defender's hand in fig. 10-1. Reverse your hand catching the opponent's gripping wrist and push your wrist against his thumb (fig. 10-2) which will distract him. Follow up with an elbow break (fig. 10-3).

Fig. 10-1

Fig. 10-2

Fig. 10-3

Joint Lock No. 2

Turn your held hand up so that the palm is facing you. Grasp your attacker's hand at the base of his thumb (fig. 10-4). Withdraw your held hand and grasp the attacker's hand in such a manner that both your thumbs are acting as pushing levers against the back of his hand and your fingers are pulling against the thumb base. This will violently twist his hand and wrist (fig. 10-5), causing his wrist to break.

Fig. 10-4

Fig. 10-5

Joint Lock No. 3

Rotate your held hand so that your opponent's wrist is trapped in the "V" of your forefinger and thumb (fig. 10-6). At the same time bring your free hand up and grasp his hand (fig. 10-7). Holding his hand closely to your body, step forward with the right foot and press down sharply with the "V." (fig. 10-8)

Fig. 10-6

Fig. 10-7

Fig. 10-8

Joint Lock No. 4

Trap your opponent's wrist in the "V" and bring your free hand across to trap his same hand in a "V" (fig. 10-9 & 10). Spin to the left and catch his elbow under your armpit (fig. 10-11). If you force the two "V's" together, making sure that they are placed on either side of the wrist joint, and snap into his elbow with your armpit, both his wrist and elbow may break.

Fig. 10-9

Fig. 10-10

Fig. 10-11

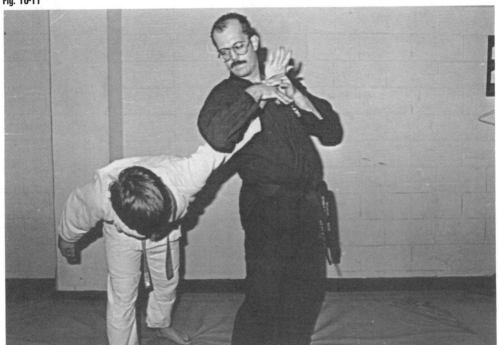

Self-Defense
Against a Held Wrist:

Throwing an assailant violently to the ground is an effective way to render him harmless or even kill him. Some of the throws in hapkido are just like the ones used in tournament judo play. Others are more like the joint breaking throws used in judo's ancestor, jujutsu. Before attempting any of the techniques in this chapter, master the basic breakfalls and make sure your partner has also.

Throw No. 1

At the instant your wrist is grabbed (fig. 11-1) rotate the held hand to the inside and clasp the attacker's wrist (fig. 11-2). Pull him forward and at the same time grab his upper sleeve and step

Fig. 11-1

in and across (fig. 11-3). Continue to turn, bringing your forearm up under his armpit (fig. 11-4) and make sure your buttocks make contact with his abdomen below the tanjon area. Maintaining a constant pull forward, straighten your legs (fig. 11-5). Bend at the waist and pull his arm across your body (fig. 11-6) which will propel him up and over your shoulder. When he hits the ground (notice the correct side breakfall position in fig. 11-7), continue to hold his wrist, and turn his arm so that his elbow is pointing towards your knee. Pull back on the arm while you kneel on the elbow (fig. 11-8). This coup de grace may be used as a submission hold or as an elbow break, depending on the situation.

Fig. 11-2

Fig. 11-3

Fig. 11-4

Fig. 11-5

71

Fig. 11-6

Fig. 11-7

Fig. 11-8

Throw No. 2

Start as in Throw No. 1 (fig. 11-9) except as you step across, bring the crook of your arm under the attacker's upper arm (fig. 11-10). As you pivot, lock the live-hand across his elbow (fig. 11-11). Straighten your legs and bring his arm across your body as you bend forward (fig. 11-12). This will throw him over and to the floor.

Fig. 11-9

Fig. 11-10

Fig. 11-11

Fig. 11-12

Cooling Down Exercise

A race horse is always walked after he has run a race and a track competitor wouldn't think of sitting down right after a strenuously run event. The same should apply for a student after a hapkido practice session. Leg and groin muscles in particular will be tired and should be stretched out to minimize the danger of cramps or strains. The following set of calisthenics, sarcastically named "calling it a day" by Major Song Ho Jin, is designed to stretch out tired muscles and to relax the student.

Cool-Down

Stand with your legs wide apart and slightly bent (fig. 12-1). Squat straight downward, forcing your breath out through the mouth and forcing your live-hands down and out (fig. 12-2 & 3). Return to the standing position, inhaling through your nose. Do ten repetitions.

Fig. 12-1

Fig. 12-2

Fig. 12-3

PART III:

Intermediate Level: Red Belt

Sweeps

There are two varieties of sweeps. The first sweep is the sit down round kick.

Sit-Down-Round Kick

This kick is one of hapkido's more dangerous weapons. It is designed to cut the legs out from under an opponent, dumping him to the ground and possibly breaking one of his legs at the same time. It starts like a round kick, with the right foot turned outside as it advances (fig. 13-1). Bring the left foot across, pivot the body, and lock over your right shoulder at your target (fig. 13-2). Lower your body over your left foot, extend your right leg, and place your hands on the floor

Fig. 13-1

Fig. 13-2

between your knees (fig. 13-3). Pivot on the ball of your left foot, pushing off with your hands, and swing your right leg all the way around in a circle parallel to the floor (fig. 13-4). You should end up back in an on-guard position (fig. 13-5). If you use it against the back of an opponent's leg, as shown in (fig. 13-6), he will be knocked into the air. Notice that the sit-down-round kick is especially effective against an attacker while he's kicking. Drop under his kick and attack his supporting leg. This is especially devastating when your kick is directed to the front of his supporting leg (fig. 13-7), since it will break his knee as well as throw him on his face.

Fig. 13-3

Fig. 13-4

Fig. 13-5

Fig. 13-6

Fig. 13-7

Sit-Down-Sweep Kick

This is another good attack. From the starting position (fig. 13-8), squat down on the ball of your forward foot, placing your hands on either side of your supporting leg (fig. 13-9). Snap your rear leg around in an arc, sweeping your opponent's front leg from behind (fig. 13-10). Attempting to aim this kick at the hard shin of an opponent, however, can result in injuries to the tendons and bones on the top of your own foot.

Fig. 13-8

Fig. 13-9

Fig. 13-10

Basic Kick Defenses

By now we have covered quite a few kicking techniques. To round out your training, you must acquire the ability to defend against these kicks.

The easiest way to block a kick is to get out of its way by moving backwards or to either side (figs. 14-1 through 4).

Fig. 14-1

Fig. 14-2

Fig. 14-3

Fig. 14-4

An excellent drill for learning how to pivot to the side to escape a kick requires a long staff or broom. Have a partner stand in front of you, pointing the stick at your chest (fig. 14-5). Stand flat-footed and relaxed. As your opponent thrusts the staff, twist your torso (fig. 14-6) and pivot quickly to the side as the staff goes by (fig. 14-7). Do this ten or twenty times to each side every practice session until you have the motion down to an instinctive reaction. Then you will be ready for the first block.

Fig. 14-5

Fig. 14-6

Fig. 14-7

Block

This block is used to guard against a front or side kick. From an on-guard position (fig. 14-8) pivot to the side bringing your forward arm down along your side to protect your ribs (fig. 14-9. The kick will pass by your body (fig. 14-10).

Fig. 14-8

Fig. 14-9

Fig. 14-10

Basic Punch Defense

The theories of one-step-and-joint and force redirection hold true for hapkido's blocking system for defending yourself against a fist attack. As in the kick defenses, the easiest defense against a punch is to get out of its way by moving backwards or sideways (fig. 15-1 through 4).

Fig. 15-1

Fig. 15-2

Fig. 15-3

Fig. 15-4

A live hand covering the face also works very well. It redirects the force of the blow and covers the target area in the same manner as a boxer takes punches on the gloves (figs. 15-5 through 7).

Fig. 15-5

Fig. 15-6

Fig. 15-7

Block

As the punch moves forward, bring your opposite hand across and up your body, while at the same time stepping to the outside of the punch (fig. 15-8). As the punch slips by your face, add to and redirect its motion by pushing the attacker's elbow down and across your body (fig. 15-9) with your free hand. This action pushes the attacker's head down and brings your blocking hand up (fig. 15-10). Then bring your hand back down with a knife-hand to his neck (fig. 15-11). Follow up with a knee kick to the attacker's body (fig. 15-12 & 13).

Fig. 15-8

Fig. 15-9

Fig. 15-10

Fig. 15-11

Fig. 15-12

Fig. 15-13

Intermediate Escapes

Intermediate escapes are more complete, while adhering to the same basic principles. Here are some examples of intermediate escapes.

Escape No. 1

Clasp the attacker's hand with your free hand and bring the live hand up (fig. 16-1) and across, holding his hand firmly (figs. 16-2 & 3), causing him extreme pain from the unnaturally twisted wrist.

Fig. 16-1

Fig. 16-2

Fig. 16-3

Escape No. 2

Similarly to Escape #1, clasp the opponent's holding hand (fig. 16-4). Bring the live hand up to the inside of his wrist, place it on the top of his wrist (fig. 16-5) and bear down and forward with it (fig. 16-6).

Fig. 16-4

Fig. 16-5

Fig. 16-6

Escape No. 3

Clasp the opponent's lower sleeve and upper sleeve, pulling him forward while you pivot (fig. 16-7) and throw him (fig. 16-8).

Fig. 16-7

Fig. 16-8

Free Sparring

If you have mastered all the techniques covered in Parts II and III, you should now be ready to learn free sparring. It is not advisable to begin this activity unless you have a good grasp of the basic hapkido movements, and have achieved some degree of self-control in applying these techniques. No one is more dangerous than the beginning martial artist because he tends to get too excited and lose control. Take care not to injure your sparring partner.

Start out slowly, especially in the beginning. Talk through the motions; pre-plan them with your partner. Don't try to kill each other your first session.

Begin and end each sparring session with a bow (fig. 17-1 & 2), the hapkidoist's version of a salute or good-will hand shake. Proper courtesy and strict discipline help keep tempers cool while free sparring. Forget about one-upmanship. Anyone who has to prove he's better is not ready for free sparring.

Fig. 17-1

Fig. 17-2

Fig. 17-3

Unlike many other martial arts, hapkido is not hung-up on a lot of "classical" stances. Use the on-guard positions that feel most comfortable to you and are easiest to move from quickly. Fig. 17-3 shows a suggested position is shown which may meet the above criteria. It also provides high, middle, and low protection. Someone attacking from the front (fig. 17-4 & 5) will find it very difficult to penetrate this defense.

Fig. 17-4

Fig. 17-5

Therefore, when opposing someone with a good on-guard position, try attacking from the sides, rather than from the direct front (fig. 17-6 through 10).

Fig. 17-6

Fig. 17-7

Fig. 17-8

Fig. 17-9

Fig. 17-10

The following candid pictures were taken during a free sparring session to give some ideas of how you can apply hapkido techniques in a fluid situation.

Jumping back-first attack (fig. 17-11).

Fig. 17-11

A back-side kick that didn't get blocked (fig. 17-12 & 13).

Fig. 17-12

Fig. 17-13

PART IV:

Advanced Level: First Degree Black Belt

Offensive Moves

So far we have addressed ourselves to mostly defensive techniques designed to counter an attack. This chapter deals with the possibility of assuming the offensive first. If you're cornered and you feel certain that someone is going to try to harm you, it makes good sense to try to get him first. There are many things you might do in a situation like that. The next three techniques are examples of some effective joint locks. Remember, there are many kicks and punches which could be used also. Experiment on your own and find out which defensive techniques work best for you as offensive moves.

Attack No. 1

Grab your opponent's wrist with both your hands (fig. 18-1) and lunge your shoulder into his elbow (fig. 18-2).

Fig. 18-1

Fig. 18-2

Attack No. 2

Turn your attacking hand over so the thumb is on the bottom (fig. 18-3). Clasp your opponent's hand on the same side with the "Vs" of your hands (fig. 18-4) and turn it back into him (fig. 18-5).

Fig. 18-3

Fig. 18-4

Fig. 18-5

Attack No. 3

Turn your attacking hand over (fig. 18-6) and grasp, across your body, the underside of your opponent's hand (fig. 18-7). Turn his hand over while clasping it with both your hands (fig. 18-8). Push his hand back toward him with your thumbs and pull his wrist towards you (fig. 18-9). Finish him off with a front kick to the face (fig. 18-10).

Fig. 18-6

Fig. 18-7

Fig. 18-8

Fig. 18-9

Fig. 18-10

Advanced Kick Defenses

The theories of spinning and one-step-and-join apply to the methods shown in this chapter, as they did to the basic kick blocks of Chapter III. However, these blocks require more timing and coordination. There are three series of advanced kick blocks: those used against the inside side and front kicks, those used against the inside and outside crescent kicks, and those used against the roundhouse kick.

Block No. 1

Catch the extended kick on your front arm (fig. 19-1) and counter with a side kick to the attacker's groin, inner thigh, or inside of the knee joint (fig. 19-2).

Fig. 19-1

Fig. 19-2

Block No. 2

Extend your crossed arms until they make contact with the attacker's leg (fig. 19-3). Don't try to stop the kick there. Ride its force till it comes close, then quickly capture his foot with your crossed hands (fig. 19-4). Pull up and counter with a front kick to his groin (fig. 19-5).

Fig. 19-3

Fig. 19-4

Fig. 19-5

Block No. 3

As his foot comes up, watch for the angle that your opponent's foot must travel (fig. 19-6), then step outside it (fig. 19-7). Catch your opponent's kicking leg and grab his upper sleeve (fig. 19-8). Step through and sweep your leg back into his knee (fig. 19-9), breaking his leg and throwing him on his face at the same time.

Fig. 19-6

Fig. 19-7

Fig. 19-8

Fig. 19-9

CHAPTER TWENTY

Advanced Punch Defenses

Like the advanced kick defenses, the advanced punch defenses take a little more coordination and timing.

Punch Block No. 1

As the attacker punches, step to the outside of the blow's path and grab the arm as it goes by (fig. 20-1 & 2). Make the grab high on the forearm so that when your hand closes, it will be around his wrist and won't slip off his hand. After grabbing his wrist, clasp his arm at the elbow with the other hand (fig. 20-3). Pivot into him while pulling at his arm and pushing on his locked wrist (fig. 20-4). Note how the defender's elbow strikes the attacker in the face as the pivot is made.

Fig. 20-1

Fig. 20-2

Fig. 20-3

Fig. 20-4

Punch Block No. 2

The next two techniques show a great deal of Chinese influence; they turn a block into a counterattack, using the blocking hand as the weapon. As the punch travels towards you, step inside and block it with the bony part of your underwrist against the attacker's inner-arm tendons (fig. 20-5 & 6). As the attacker's blow travels by your face (fig. 20-7), counterattack with a chicken-hand to the soft facial bones (fig. 20-8). Flick your finger tips into his eyes (fig. 20-9) and draw the attacking hand back (fig. 20-10) in preparation for a heel-of-the-hand blow to his groin (fig. 20-11) to rupture his bladder.

Fig. 20-5

Fig. 20-6

Fig. 20-7

Fig. 20-8

Fig. 20-9

Fig. 20-10

Fig. 20-11

Defenses While Sitting or Lying Down

If you are ever threatened while you are seated or if you've been thrown to the ground, don't think that all is lost. There are several ways of protecting yourself.

Seated Defense No. 1

If you are seated and an attacker comes Up (fig. 21-1), simply grasp his forward ankle (fig. 21-2) and place a live-hand hardened forearm against the front of his shin (fig. 21-3). Pull his foot to you while pressing forward and down with your arm. This is surprisingly painful!

Fig. 21-1

Fig. 21-2

Fig. 21-3

Seated Defense No. 2

Grab behind the attacker's ankle and place the palm of your hand against his knee (fig. 21-4). Pull the ankle and push the knee at the same time (fig. 21-5).

Fig. 21-4

Fig. 21-5

Seated Defense No. 3

Grab your opponent's ankle and push against the inside of his knee toward the outside (fig. 21-6 & 7).

Fig. 21-6

Fig. 21-7

Seated Defense No. 4

If the attacker grabs a handful of your hair while you are seated (fig. 21-8), clasp his hand to your head and clasp you own wrist under his arm (fig. 21-9). Quickly rotate your head and hands down and to the inside (fig. 21-10), breaking his wrist.

Fig. 21-8

Fig. 21-9

Fig. 21-10

Seated Defense No. 5

If you are lying down and your attacker approaches you from the front, sweep his front leg from behind (fig. 21-11 through 13).

Fig. 21-11

Fig. 21-12

Fig. 21-13

Seated Defense No. 6

You can also use the position shown in (fig. 21-14) to break his knee by hooking behind his front foot with your bottom foot (fig. 21-15) and kicking forward with your upper foot (fig. 21-16).

Fig. 21-14

Fig. 21-15

Fig. 21-16

Cross Wrist Escapes

Use the basic principles learned at the lower belt levels to escape from a person holding your wrist (fig. 22-1).

Fig. 22-1

Wrist Escape No. 1

A simple and effective escape is to clasp the holding hand to your wrist and bring your live hand up (fig. 22-2) and around to rest on your attacker's wrist (fig. 22-3). Press both your hands down, putting considerable strain on the attacker's wrist (fig. 22-4). Figs. 22-5 & 6 show this strain from a different angle.

Fig. 22-2

Fig. 22-3

Fig. 22-4

Fig. 22-5

147

Fig. 22-6

Wrist Escape No. 2

From the starting position (fig. 22-7) rotate your held hand to the outside as you step outside (fig. 22-8). Break your opponent's arm with your hardened forearm (fig. 22-9).

Fig. 22-7

Fig. 22-8

Fig. 22-9

Defenses Against a Club Attack

The secret to defending yourself from a swinging club is to get inside the weapon's arc. Since the club's power is diminished once you get inside, you can control the attacker's movements and counter with less danger to yourself.

Club Defense No. 1

If your attacker comes at you with a roundhouse swing (fig. 23-1), meet it with the near-side hand (fig. 23-2) and bring up your other arm with a live hand behind his upper arm. Try to cross two arms(fig. 23-3). This will break his elbow with the help of his own momentum.

Fig. 23-1

Fig. 23-2

Fig. 23-3

Club Defense No. 2

If the attacker swings back-handed (fig. 23-4), catch his wrist as it descends (fig. 23-5), turn his hand palm up and break his elbow as you throw (fig. 23-6 & 7).

Fig. 23-4

Fig. 23-5

Fig. 23-6

Fig. 23-7

Defense Against Knife Attacks

If you're ever confronted by an assailant with a knife, keep your cool and don't panic. Remember, you have many weapons on your body and, if you use these well, you can take his away from him. Think positively! Don't worry about the possibility of getting cut. Assume that it may happen and make him pay the price before he can get you.

Knife Defense No. 1

If your assailant holds the knife loosely in front of himself (fig. 24-1), snap a front kick into his hand and wrist (fig. 24-2), causing the knife to fly out of his hand and over his shoulder.

Fig. 24-1

Fig. 24-2

Knife Defense No. 2

If he lunges with the knife held low (fig. 24-3), meet it with both hands at the early part of his movement (fig. 24-4) and pivot under his arm (fig. 24-5). Pull the knife back into his stomach to complete the circle (fig. 24-6).

Fig. 24-3

Fig. 24-4

157

Fig. 24-5

Fig. 24-6

Knife Defense No. 3

An alternate method is to meet the knife arm (fig. 24-7), bring it in a circle across your body and spin under it (fig. 24-8). Pull the knife hand straight down (fig. 24-9). If your attacker drops the knife — and he should —you can pick it up and use it on him (fig. 24-10).

Fig. 24-7

Fig. 24-8

Fig. 24-9

Fig. 24-10

Countering Throws

If your assailant attempts a throw on you (fig. 25-1 & 2), flow your ki low and squat slightly (fig. 25-3). This will put your attacker off balance and he'll find it impossible to throw you. If he makes the mistake of not getting in close enough when he pivots inside (fig. 25-4), shoot your leg through and execute a hip roll, using his back as a fulcrum (fig. 25-5 & 6).

Fig. 25-1

Fig. 25-2

Fig. 25-3

Fig. 25-4

Fig. 25-5

Fig. 25-6

Escape From Chokes

Choke Escape No. 1

Here's how to counter one of the most common attacks: If an enraged assailant stands face to face with you and wraps both his hands around your throat (fig. 26-1), grab his lapels with one hand and push against his chin with your other (fig. 26-2 through 4).

Fig. 26-1

Fig. 26-2

Fig. 26-3

Fig. 26-4

164

Choke Escape No. 2

Another effective counter is to shove a live hand down through his arms (fig. 26-5) and bend over until he releases his grip (fig. 26-6). Then come back up with your elbow and strike every target of opportunity on the arc of the upward swing (fig. 26-7 & 8). This works very well for women since it pits one's entire body weight against the assailant's wrists.

Fig. 26-5

Fig. 26-6

Fig. 26-7

Fig. 26-8

Choke Escape No. 3

If an attacker grabs you from behind with a neck breaker (fig. 26-9), tuck your chin into his elbow crook. Then reach back, grab a finger and pull it down (fig. 26-10 & 11).

Fig. 26-9

Fig. 26-10

Fig. 26-11

PART V

Upper Belt Level Familiarization

Cane and Umbrella (Stick) Techniques

If you are ever attacked and happen to have a cane or umbrella handy, relax. These common everyday items can be lethal weapons in the hapkidoist's hands. You can use the point, the shaft, or the crook to defend yourself. However, the umbrella's shaft is too weak to strike effective blows, although it may be used to block.

Stick Technique No. 1

Figs. 27-1 through 27-7 demonstrate how you can use the shaft to block a punch and the point to attack the face, throat, or midsection of your opponent.

Fig. 27-1

Fig. 27-2

Fig. 27-3

Fig. 27-4

Fig. 27-5

171

Fig. 27-6

Fig. 27-7

Stick Technique No. 2

Block the punch to the outside (fig. 27-8), circle the cane (figs. 27-9 & 10), and strike behind the knee (fig. 27-11).

Fig. 27-8

Fig. 27-9

Fig. 27-10

Fig. 27-11

Fighting Stick Familiarization

Another lethal weapon in the hapkido inventory is a stick twelve inches long, one inch in diameter, made of hard wood. It can be used like a policeman's night-stick, like a Japanese konga or yawara stick, and in ways unique to hapkido. Its shaft may be used for striking and blocking. Its ends may also be used. Figs. 28-1 through 28-6 show how to make an overhand strike with the shaft. Notice the amount of wrist play. This is to ensure maximum snap is achieved. Also note the circular motion of the delivery.

Fig. 28-1

Fig. 28-2

Fig. 28-3

Fig. 28-4

Fig. 28-5

Fig. 28-6

Figs. 28-7 through 10 show the side arm strike. Again, snap-power is emphasized, as it is in the back-hand strike shown in figs. 28-11 through 14.

Side Arm Strike

Fig. 28-7

Fig. 28-8

Fig. 28-9

Fig. 28-10

Back-Hand Strike

Fig. 28-11

Fig. 28-12

Fig. 28-13

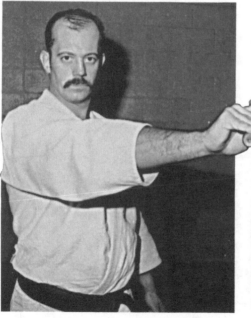

Fig. 28-14

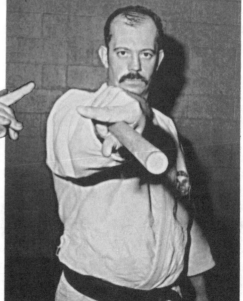

Figs. 28-15 & 16 demonstrate striking with the tip of the stick.

Fig. 28-15

Fig. 28-16

Figs. 28-17 through 21 picture several of the many possible positions used for blocking.

Fig. 28-17

Fig. 28-18

Fig. 28-19

Fig. 28-20

Fig. 28-21

Figs. 28-22 through 28-26 show the side-arm strike in action against an opponent's neck.

Fig. 28-22

Fig. 28-23

Fig. 28-24

Fig. 28-25

Fig. 28-26

Figs. 28-27 through 29 demonstrate the use of the back-hand strike to block a punch and temporarily paralyze the tendons of the opponent's inner wrist.

Fig. 28-27

Fig. 28-28

Fig. 28-29

About the Author

Robert Spear is the first American to attain a third degree black belt in the Republic of Korea from the Korea Hapkido Association; he is also the first American to receive a letter of certification as an instructor from that same association. Spear is a 5th Dan member of the U.S. Hapkido Federation and the Midori Yama Budokai Association.

An ex-army intelligence officer, Spear has taught combat fighting and self-defense to soldiers in Korea and the U.S. as well as to civilians in Arizona and Kansas. Spear has evaluated electronic warfare systems for the army since 1976. Military tactics instructors at the U.S. Army's Command and General Staff College at Fort Leavenworth, Kansas, have used his martial art theories to create new tactics and strategies. He is currently an Army civil servant in Europe.

A recognized martial art theorist, Spear has presented papers on the arts at the 1984 Olympic Scientific Congress and the American Association for Fitness in Business. A feature article, "Bushido in the Boardroom," on his theory of Universal Force Dynamics, was published in Rodale Press' *Executive Fitness Newsletter*. Spear is also the president and chief consultant for his business/governmental consulting firm, Universal Force Dynamics, Inc.

Spear holds an M.S. in business management from the University of Northern Colorado and a B.S. in both music and business from Indiana University. He is a member of the intellectual societies Mensa and Intertel.